RASHMA N. KALSIE is an Indian writer-playwright based in Australia. She is the founder of Indian Diaspora Dramatics Association. Rashma's work includes the plays *Padma Shri Prahasana* (India Habitat Centre, Delhi), *The Day I Left Home—Melbourne Talam* (MTC NEON Readings 2015, MTC Cybec Electric Festival 2016), *The Lost Dog* (Walker Gallery & Arts Centre 2012 and 2014), *The Rejected Girl* (Mumbai Theatre Guide One-Act Plays Shortlist) and *Meri Script Hai Kahan* (Eventura Creations 2003); the novels *Ohh! Gods are Online* (Srishti Publishers & Distributors) and *The Buddha and the Bitch* (Purple Folio); and over 100 scripts for TV shows with B.A.G. Films and News and Entertainment Television. She has published articles and shorts in print and online magazines—*Woman's Era, Manushi*, garamchai.com and feminafastfiction.com. Rashma studied TV Journalism from Academy 18 (a school of TV18), Screenwriting from University of Toronto, Playwrights' Workshop (Mahesh Dattani and India Habitat Centre), and Natyashastra Workshop (Dr Bharat Gupt). Rashma is an AWG Associate Member.

Photo by Karanvir Singh.

MELBOURNE TALAM

RASHMA N. KALSIE

Currency Press, Sydney

CURRENCY PLAYS

First published in 2017
by Currency Press Pty Ltd,
PO Box 2287, Strawberry Hills, NSW, 2012, Australia
enquiries@currency.com.au
www.currency.com.au

in association with Melbourne Theatre Company

Copyright: *Melbourne Talam* © Rashma N. Kalsie, 2017.

COPYING FOR EDUCATIONAL PURPOSES

The Australian *Copyright Act 1968* (Act) allows a maximum of one chapter or 10% of this book, whichever is the greater, to be copied by any educational institution for its educational purposes provided that that educational institution (or the body that administers it) has given a remuneration notice to Copyright Agency Limited (CAL) under the Act.

For details of the CAL licence for educational institutions contact CAL, 11/66 Goulburn Street, Sydney, NSW, 2000; tel: within Australia 1800 066 844 toll free; outside Australia 61 2 9394 7600; fax: 61 2 9394 7601; email: info@copyright.com.au

COPYING FOR OTHER PURPOSES

Except as permitted under the Act, for example a fair dealing for the purposes of study, research, criticism or review, no part of this book may be reproduced, stored in a retrieval system, or transmitted in any form or by any means without prior written permission. All enquiries should be made to the publisher at the address above.

Any performance or public reading of *Melbourne Talam* is forbidden unless a licence has been received from the author or the author's agent. The purchase of this book in no way gives the purchaser the right to perform the play in public, whether by means of a staged production or a reading. All applications for public performance should be addressed to the author c/- Currency Press.

Cataloguing-in-publication data for this title is available from the National Library of Australia website: www.nla.gov.au

Typeset by Dean Nottle for Currency Press.
Cover design by Emma Wagstaff.

Currency Press acknowledges the Traditional Owners of the Country on which we live and work. We pay our respects to all Aboriginal and Torres Strait Islander Elders, past and present.

Contents

MELBOURNE TALAM

    Act One   1

    Act Two   31

PLAYWRIGHT'S NOTE

Melbourne Talam has been three years in the writing, growing with every draft and with every person who has been part of its journey. Scores of people have contributed their stories and insights during its long development. Indian students at La Trobe and RMIT University, SBS Punjabi journalists, Indian taxi drivers, Carnatic musicians, Telugu-speaking friends, Indian friends in Melbourne and my younger brother Rocky, who came to Melbourne as a student, have all helped shape the play.

Melbourne Talam is the story of Melbourne as much as it's the story of three Indians who dream of making Melbourne home. Every city has its own rhythm or *talam* (Carnatic music). An outsider/migrant must learn to sync their life with the rhythm of their adopted city or their life goes off-key. I have tried to paint the city of Melbourne in Indian colours. We hear, see and experience Melbourne as Sonali, Jasminder and Poorna try to find their *talam* in the city. We see glimpses of their homes and Indian cities. They are looking for love, money, job, friends, someone to talk to or even a corner in a room. Like God, Melbourne gives with one hand and takes away with the other.

I am grateful to MTC and Chris Mead for the insights and the opportunities they provided for the script to develop.

Rashma N. Kalsie

Melbourne Talam was first produced by Melbourne Theatre Company at Southbank Theatre, Lawler Studio, Melbourne, on 4 May 2017, with the following cast:

JASMINDER	Rohan Mirchandaney
POORNA	Sahil Saluja
SONALI	Sonya Suares

Director, Petra Kalive
Set and Costume Designer, Andrew Bailey
Lighting Designer, Rachel Burke
Composer and Sound Designer, Darius Kedros
Movement Director, Lyndall Grant

Melbourne Talam was presented as a staged reading at MTC's 2015 NEON Readings in association with MTC CONNECT—a partnership with Multicultural Arts Victoria—and at MTC Cybec Electric 2016, directed by Alex Pinder and read by Rayesh Gunasekera, Sahil Saluja and Suhasini Seelin.

CHARACTERS

SONALI CHUGH, 29

POORNACHANDRA RAO [POORNA], 24

JASMINDER SINGH, 19

Multiple minor characters are shared between the three actors who play the above main roles. These characters are (in order of appearance): INTERVIEWER, SONALI'S BROTHER, VIVEK, PASSENGERS (2), SHASHI, BOSS, GIRL, RAGESHWARI, MOHIT, PARMINDER, JASMINDER'S MOTHER, SARABJIT SINGH, RANBEER, POORNA'S MOTHER, ANDREW, TEACHER, IMMIGRATION AGENT, JASMINDER'S FATHER, AUSTRALIAN MAN, LANDLADY, SONALI'S MOTHER, RICKY, MARTHA, SONALI'S FATHER, and NURSE.

SETTING

Melbourne Talam is a play that exists both in imagination and on the streets, offices, hospitals, apartments, tram stops and train stations of Melbourne and is painted as much through stage action as the recesses of the mind. Melbourne is not only a city where protagonists live but it is a living character with many faces. The play uses elements of presentational and representational theatre to tell the many stories and the audience completes the play by putting together the pieces of the puzzle.

Talam (Tamil) or *tala* (Sanskrit) is a term used in Indian music. *Talam* is the base on which the notes of musical compositions and poetry rest. It is the rhythmic cycle of a musical composition. In the context of the play *talam* means the rhythm of Melbourne.

ACT ONE

SCENE ONE

Melbourne, Flagstaff Station, a weekday evening.

An announcement is in progress. A train is ready to depart in a few minutes from the crowded platform.

POORNACHANDRA RAO (24) gets off the escalator onto the platform. White sandalwood tika *on his forehead and generous coconut oil in his hair confirm he's a South Indian Brahmin.*

POORNA: Is that my train?

> *He walks up to the train, studies the information scrolling on the train.*

Huurst bridge—that's not mine, thank God. Let me check the TV screen.

> *He goes up to the display monitor, scans it. His umbrella is dripping. He shakes it, spraying water all over.*

Ah, there's plenty of time for my train. Now I can relax.

> *He sits down on a seat.*

I could have taken the earlier train if I had walked faster but I was enjoying Carnatic music in my mother's voice.

> *He inserts earphones, switches on music on his phone.*

Aah! *'Vathapi Ganpathim'* ... I recorded this when *amma* was doing her morning *practice*. All my life I have woken up to this song.

[*Singing*] *Vathapi Ganpathim bhajeham*
  Vathapi Ganpathim bhajeham
  Vathapi Ganpathim bhajeham
  Vathapi Ganpathim bhajeham
  Vaaranaasyam Vara Pradham Sri
  Vaaranaasyam Vara Pradham Sri ...

> POORNA *claps the song on his thigh in Carnatic tradition.*

A passenger announcement for a platform change.

POORNA *does not hear the announcement.*

SONALI CHUGH *(29) walks to the platform like she's walking on a ramp. She looks glamorous and attractive. The swing of her hips can be seen from a mile. She scans the platform. Looks at* POORNA, *shakes her head in disgust.*

SONALI: Where are the hot *Australian* boys?

JASMINDER SINGH *(19) runs down the stairs onto the platform. He bumps into* SONALI, *mutters an apology, and runs after the train departing from the platform.* JASMINDER*'s clothes hang on his frail body and his turban looks big on his boyish face. He is drenched.*

JASMINDER: Sorry ...

JASMINDER *wipes his running nose on his sleeve as he chases the train to the end of the platform.*

SONALI: Ugh! He stinks! I bet he hasn't washed his jacket in years.

She wipes her sweater with a tissue paper and throws the paper on the platform.

What's the big fun of living in Australia if you have to travel with the Indian men, and such substandard Indian men at that.

JASMINDER *stops running, watches the train disappear.* POORNA *looks at him with sympathy.*

JASMINDER: *O teri* ...

POORNA: *Arere*, this poor Sikh fellow—didn't get his *talam* right. [*With a sigh*] Life in Melbourne is like *talam* in Carnatic music—you have to time it right. If you follow the beats of the city, your life never goes off-key here. We Hyderabadis have our own sweet rhythm—slooow and eeeasyyy.

[*Singing*] *Vathapi Ganpathim bhajeham*
    Vathapi Ganpathim bhajeham ...

SONALI *gives* POORNA *a dirty look.* JASMINDER *is still standing, catching his breath.*

JASMINDER: *Kya yaar!* I almost got it—a few seconds and I would have been on the train. When's the next one ...?

ACT ONE

He runs to the display monitor.

Ten minutes! *Aa ki siyapa hai*—how will I reach the class on time! Twenty minutes on the train—ten minutes in the bus—twenty minutes walk—even if I run I can't make it. I can manage the other subjects but calculus is so tough. Travelling was so much easier in Gurdaspur—I used to travel by shared auto-rickshaws that *wait* for the passengers and then drop them at their doorstep. Not like Melbourne where you have to take a train to reach a bus which drops you two kilometres away from your destination.

He sneezes.

SONALI *is tired, sits down. Takes off her shoes, rests her feet on the shoes.*

SONALI: These heels are shit. I should have worn flats—it was a crazy day—customers were walking in and out and girls want to try on a hundred dresses before they buy one. I was on my knees all day, picking up dresses and hanging them back. My feet need a good massage. That's the only thing I miss here—Kantabai's massage. I wish we could bring our *servants* along.

POORNA *examines the platform, goes up to the yellow line, careful to not cross it. He checks if the train is coming from the opposite direction.*

POORNA: Where's my train?

He strolls to the display monitor, studies the information.

Arere, they changed platforms. *O Bhagwan*, where's platform four?

Beat.

He looks around to ask—no-one is looking in his direction.

Let me get out of here first. In Hyderabad you only have to look confused and people come running to help you.

He exits to the escalator. He trips on his umbrella. SONALI *is watching.*

Arere ... even the umbrellas are so difficult to manage here.

SONALI: Why do they allow such jokers into Australia?

JASMINDER *paces up and down the platform, away from* SONALI.

JASMINDER: I shouldn't have gone for the interview. Within five minutes of entering the room I knew he was going to reject me.

FLASHBACK

Melbourne, an office, morning, the same day.

INTERVIEWER: Are you an international student?

JASMINDER: Yes, sir.

CUT TO THE PRESENT

JASMINDER: And then he said something I didn't understand.

FLASHBACK

INTERVIEWER: How did you hear about this position?

JASMINDER *smiles.*

CUT TO THE PRESENT

JASMINDER: So I smiled.

FLASHBACK

INTERVIEWER: How did you hear about this position?

CUT TO THE PRESENT

JASMINDER: I realised I had to do more than smiling so I said, 'Sure'.

FLASHBACK

INTERVIEWER: Did you say sure?

CUT TO THE PRESENT

JASMINDER: Feeling more confident than before I said, 'Yes, I am sure'.

FLASHBACK

INTERVIEWER: Do you understand English?

CUT TO THE PRESENT

JASMINDER: I didn't get the job.

> JASMINDER *sits down on the seat* POORNA *has vacated. The sound of an approaching train.*

SONALI: I hope there's an adventure waiting on the train—a really exciting adventure like Ricky was—locking eyes, exchanging numbers, passionate dates, *marriage*! Yes!

She puts on her shoes, pulls down her top to reveal cleavage, walks to the train, swinging her hips. Alights.

POORNA *comes back running, confused whether he should first check the train or the display monitor. Goes to the monitor, studies it.*

POORNA: Not to worry, there's another train in ten minutes from this very platform. I'll wait next to this TV, just in case they change platforms again.

JASMINDER *has been watching him.*

JASMINDER: *Nya kabutar deesda hai*—a new pigeon from South India …

He chuckles.

SCENE TWO

Sonali's living room, night, the same day.

SONALI *limps into the messy room. She throws her bag down, sits on the couch, kicks off her shoes.*

SONALI: God, I am so tired … just want to grab a bite and sleep …

She finds a packet of bhujia, rips it open, eats a mouthful.

This fried *bhujia* is totally addictive—you can't stop until you've finished the whole packet. I didn't eat this shit in India—we had a cook and a fleet of servants who cooked three meals a day.

She picks up a bottle of wine.

I don't trust my second-hand fridge—better finish the wine before it goes bad.

She drinks.

Just what I need after a long day. I hadn't tasted wine before I came here. Girls are not allowed to drink in our family—no drinks, no short skirts, and *no boyfriends*. Except me, all the girls in the family have had to settle for an arranged marriage. They had *no* takers—

all the boys were after me. One of my cousins is getting married to an ugly billionaire. She's happy, it's the easiest way to become rich. The whole family's shopping for the wedding and posting their photos on Instagram, but my cousin's the limit.

She scrolls on her phone.

She posts her photos every ten minutes—Jeez! She's looking ugly in her red *lehenga,* and the number of likes she's got. People are so disingenuous on social media. My red *lehenga*'s so much better and my picture got 287 likes. I had worn it on my engagement. We had so much fun on my wedding—there was nonstop music, dance, party and *masti* for one whole week.

FLASHBACK

A wedding party in Delhi. Young boys and girls are dancing to a medley of Bollywood numbers—fast cuts between the songs.

CUT TO THE PRESENT

SONALI: Ttt. [*With a sigh*] I really wanted to attend my cousin's wedding but uncle hasn't invited me. He says I am a bad influence on other girls. My mother requested my cousin to invite me unofficially, like she's inviting her friends, but she refused—Bitch! My mother's so upset—I hope she's not pleading with my grandfather again. I have to stop *ma* before she makes me a laughing stock.

SONALI *calls her parents' house in Delhi.* SONALI'S BROTHER *(26) takes the call.*

I call my mother and my brother takes the call— [*On the phone*] It's me, Sonali. Where is—?

BROTHER *is playing a video game on PlayStation.*

BROTHER: Ma's not home.
SONALI: Don't cut me short.
BROTHER: I'm busy.
SONALI: Busy with what—Candy Crush!
BROTHER: Candy Crush does not affect my mother's sanity.
SONALI: Don't get our mother into this.
BROTHER: I can't leave her out, I live with her.

ACT ONE 7

SONALI: Really? You're fixated to your PlayStation—how does that help *ma's* depression?
BROTHER: I am finding myself which is better than finding men to have extramarital affairs with.
SONALI: You are so bloody Indian—always that mean Indian mentality of insulting others.
BROTHER: And what are you—Australian?
SONALI: Things happen—people fall in love.
BROTHER: You mean people fall in and out of lust.
SONALI: Vivek and I had lost our spark.
BROTHER: Maybe you should marry a fire cracker next time.
SONALI: What do you know about love and marriage, you just sit there—
BROTHER: *Dekh aisa hai*—I know what you are after. You can fool your mother with your sob stories, but you can't fool us.
SONALI: Unlike you, I earn for myself.
BROTHER: You can't afford your lifestyle, *bahna*.
SONALI: *Accha*, so you have a right to our parents' money because you are a son.
BROTHER: Monali gets what she wants—she doesn't even have to ask. *Tu rakh na.*

    BROTHER *disconnects the call.*

SONALI: *Kamina.* He thinks he can spit in my face because I made *one* mistake. Everybody makes mistakes, but my family is so unforgiving. My father is still angry I dropped out of college. I hated History, I slept through the lectures, I didn't want to waste my time doing something I didn't like, so I stopped going to college. I know it's good to have a degree, but it's my family—they oppose everything I do. They even opposed my marriage to Vivek. 'Vivek is not rich', said my father. But I liked Vivek, and more than Vivek I liked the idea of moving to Australia. And really, if they thought Vivek was a mistake they should have been happy when I divorced him, but they had a *huge* problem with my divorce. Tttt … I know I shouldn't have had an affair with Ricky whilst I was still married to Vivek but—okay, that was *one* mistake, but I corrected my mistake and moved in with Ricky. And now my family thinks Ricky was the *biggest* mistake of my life. At least I had the courage to end my marriage. I was clean—one man at a time, Ricky in, Vivek out.

Besides, I was bored with Vivek. There were no beaches, no wine, no parties, no kangaroos, not even Australian friends. We stayed at home and ...

FLASHBACK

Vivek's living room, sixteen months earlier.

VIVEK *(26) is clearing dishes from the table.* SONALI *watches.*

VIVEK: Come on, *jaan*, we'll do the dishes together. I scrub, you rinse. It'll be fun.

SONALI: That's not my idea of fun, Vivek.

VIVEK: *Arrey baba*, don't do the dishes if you don't want to, but what's your idea of fun?

SONALI: I don't know—but, why do you always invite these Indians on the weekends?

VIVEK: They are my friends, *jaan*.

SONALI: I want to go out, have fun. Only old, jaded couples spend Friday evenings at home.

VIVEK: We don't have money for pubs, *jaan*. Remember, we are saving to buy a house—home sweet home.

SONALI: I'll be *old* and arthritic by the time you buy a 'home sweet home'.

CUT TO THE PRESENT

SONALI: Vivek was a misfit. He couldn't get into the rhythm of Melbourne. I belong here—Australia is the country of my *soul*. Some people can't dance to the beat of the city—but my family doesn't understand this. I don't care if I am not invited to family weddings, at least I am free to live and love. And *love, I will*.

   SONALI *swigs wine from the bottle.*

SCENE THREE

Melbourne, evening, the same day.

POORNA *is on the train. Other* PASSENGERS *are either texting or calling.*

POORNA: Finally I am on the train. Travelling is a bit complicated in Melbourne—platform changes and all the running around ... [*sighing with relief*] but now I can relax.

ACT ONE

He watches the PASSENGERS. *But they do not notice him.*
Beat.
Melbourne people are so busy—no time to look up from their phones.
Beat.
Silence.
I'm not used to so much silence—this train is quieter than my home in Hyderabad. You can't imagine the noise in our house—old gramophone records, guitar, *tambura*, classical music, metal, rock, *Tollywood* songs, Bollywood songs, cricket commentary, news telecasts, TV serials, nonstop noise. We Hyderabadis love to talk—our buses roar with noise.

FLASHBACK
Hyderabad, back in the day.
A crowded bus. The PASSENGERS *are loud and boisterous. A* MALE PASSENGER *is listening to cricket commentary on his transistor radio.* POORNA *is trying to catch snatches of the commentary. A* FEMALE PASSENGER *is irritated by the* MALE PASSENGER *and his radio. Crowd noise from the radio.*

POORNA: Is that a boundary or a six?!
MALE PASSENGER: Hit wicket …
POORNA: *Arere,* Kohli is not focussing on cricket. We'll lose the match because of his girlfriend.
MALE PASSENGER: Don't get emotional, *young man*, all the matches are fixed.
FEMALE PASSENGER: [*sarcastic*] Not the World Cup!
MALE PASSENGER: My nephew's working in the *Deccan Chronicle*, madam, I am knowing things not known to the common man.
FEMALE PASSENGER: Married or still searching?
MALE PASSENGER: Searching, madam, searching hard. Boys having too many demands these days.
FEMALE PASSENGER: I have a niece, twenty-two years old only, verrry beautiful.
POORNA: Indians can fix anything on a bus—even your niece's arranged marriage.
MALE PASSENGER: Can I have your visiting card, madam?

CUT TO THE PRESENT

Melbourne, back on the train.

PASSENGERS *are still on their phones.* POORNA *looks at them in anticipation of a chat. He tries to say something but stops. They take no notice of him.*

Beat.

POORNA: It's alright if they don't want to talk to me. I am a happy *outsider*, under no pressure to fit in. Though we came here with a lot of preparation—we even tried to learn Australian slang on YouTube. Shashi forwarded 'How to talk Australian' videos—but no-one's called me 'shit-for-brains wanker', not yet at least. Shashi has already got into the rhythm of Melbourne. He's helping Shiva and me adjust here. We are in Melbourne to work on a project—software development and IT stuff. We are fast friends—Shashi, Shiva and me. We were having good fun up until last week …

FLASHBACK

Melbourne CBD, an office, a few days ago.

SHASHI *(25) and* POORNA *are with the* BOSS *(36). She is cold and artificial. You cannot read her mind—her expression remains constant.*

BOSS: I have news for you—good and bad.
SHASHI: Can we have the bad news first?
BOSS: We lost the contract you had been hired for.
SHASHI: What the—shit!
POORNA: Do you want us to go back to Hyderabad?
BOSS: That's the good news—we'll make a place for one guy—the best guy stays in Melbourne, others go back to Hyderabad.

CUT TO THE PRESENT

POORNA: It's a great career opportunity. I'll learn a lot if I get the job, but I don't connect with anything in this city. Not even the girls—they are too tall for me. Besides, I have a girl in Hyderabad—Rageshwari! Her office is on the third floor, mine's on the seventh. I used to wait for her outside the lift so that we could go up together. We have been talking—*na*, not talking, just wishing each other good morning for three months. Yes, only a good morning. Now that's something I admire here—you like a girl, you start talking, then you go dating and then bang-bang. Indian girls are slow. They will talk to you after you have followed them around for a month and two months after the first hello they'll drop the bomb.

FLASHBACK

Hyderabad, back in the day.

GIRL: Hi—my wedding card. He lives in the US.

POORNA: And you'll be thinking what's she so happy about—going to the US or marrying her aunt's neighbour's nephew's son? Why can't these girls tell you right at the start. So I asked Rageshwari, 'Are you by any chance engaged to a distant cousin in the US?'

RAGESHWARI *(22) giggles.*

She giggled all the way to the third floor. Even the lift operator knows. He winks at me when we are alone *arerre* ... my station—*Agu*!

POORNA *runs to the door. The* PASSENGERS *do not react.*

Stop stop stop stop stop ... *O bhagwan*, I missed my *talam* again.

SCENE FOUR

Melbourne, Jasminder's studio flat, night, the same day,

MOHIT *(21) and* PARMINDER *(22) are sleeping on the floor. They are curled up under their blankets. There are two vacant mattresses on the floor.*

JASMINDER *barges into the room from the toilet. Switches on the light.*

JASMINDER: I come home after a long day and I can't even use the toilet, someone's vomited on the floor. Ranbeer's doing night shift, it has to be—bloody Mohit! *Saale teri tou* ...

He pulls the blanket off MOHIT. MOHIT *resists.*

Chheti uth—get up and clean your muck.

MOHIT *pulls up his blanket.*

MOHIT: Pleeease ... I am sick.

JASMINDER: Sick, *teri maa ki* ... *Uth*—I can smell your puke here, you bloody alcoholic.

MOHIT: Not now, not now ...

JASMINDER: Where do you want me to pee? This is not Punjab where you can pee in the streets.
MOHIT: Shhh!

>JASMINDER *kicks* MOHIT.

>*He lies down on his mattress, but does not take off his jacket. He tosses in bed.*

JASMINDER: *Saali yeh*—how can anyone sleep on this damp mattress, it's old and worn out.
MOHIT: Switch off the light, *yaar*—I am sick.
JASMINDER: You think you are sick …

>*He grabs* MOHIT*'s hand, brings it to his forehead.*

Can you feel the heat … do you think my fever's over a hundred and two?

>MOHIT *wakes up but does not sit up.* JASMINDER *takes out a strip of medicine from his jacket.*

I have the medicine for fever but it's past expiry date, do you think I can still have it?

>JASMINDER *tries to show him the medicine.*

MOHIT: *Try kar le.*

>MOHIT *does not look at the medicine, slips under the blanket.*

JASMINDER: *Tu so*—just go back to sleep … *Saala* useless fellow. Let me have it anyway. I have to leave in four hours for work, I need rest before I can start again. Studies *and the newspaper wallah* job is killing me …

>*He swallows the medicine. Switches off the light, sits on a chair.*

This chair's so much better than my bed. I had picked my mattress off the street. Ranbeer allows only slim mattresses in the flat. My mattress is perfect for the room, but it is sagging now—maybe it's the moisture in the air. If I put it out in the sun it just might come back to its original shape. Sleeping on the floor is not a problem—I am used to it. Sarabjit uncle, my father's younger brother, used to come down from London to attend the weddings of our relatives. Uncle and his family were given the cots, whereas we slept on the floor. *Bebe*, my mother would say:

ACT ONE 13

FLASHBACK
Gurdaspur, back in the day.
JASMINDER'S MOTHER *(50) with a young* JASMINDER.
JASMINDER'S MOTHER: They are our guests, Jassi—they are not used to hardships.

CUT TO THE PRESENT
JASMINDER: So I thought life is *easier* abroad. Sarabjit uncle had run away from home after fighting with my grandfather. Nobody knew where he was for ten years and then suddenly he returned with a suitcase full of gifts.

FLASHBACK
Gurdaspur, back in the day.
SARABJIT SINGH *(53) is sitting on a cot with an open suitcase, displaying gifts to* JASMINDER'S MOTHER. *He exhibits a shirt.*
SARABJIT: *Ae Jassi layii*. My son has worn it only *five* times. We bought it from Marks & Spencer *behenji*—a *big* store in London. Jassi can wear it on his birthday.
JASMINDER'S MOTHER: *Jassi da birthday te lang gaya prahji*—we celebrated last month.
SARABJIT: *O mainu sab pata hai*, it's a gift for his next birthday …

CUT TO THE PRESENT
JASMINDER *brings his blanket on the chair.*
JASMINDER: Sarabjit uncle is the hero of our family. He has seen the whole world and he drives a BMW. Uncle owns a big business in London, but there have been all sorts of rumours about him—someone from our village had seen Sarabjit uncle at Heathrow airport. He claims uncle was cleaning toilets! I don't believe him—people are jealous of Sarabjit uncle's success. How can a janitor buy a BMW? Bauji, my father, retired as the head postmaster of Gurdaspur, but he can't afford a BMW. He drives a scooter. Bauji could have bought a small car if he didn't have to pay my fees. We were hoping the money we got from selling our farm would pay for the entire course, but I've run out of it in eighteen months. Fourth semester fees are due in five weeks. I called my mother yesterday …

FLASHBACK
The previous day.

JASMINDER *is on the phone with his* MOTHER.

JASMINDER'S MOTHER: Bauji's trying, *putr*. Had he been working in the post office he would have easily got a bank loan.

JASMINDER: Why are you wasting time—just go for a private loan. I need the money in five weeks, *bebe*—we will lose everything if you don't send me money on time.

JASMINDER'S MOTHER: Private lenders want an assurance, son, we've already sold the farm.

JASMINDER: But we have our *house*.

JASMINDER'S MOTHER: It's your grandmother's house, we can't mortgage it against her will. You know how she feels about the house.

JASMINDER: Just explain to her the house is safe. Once I find a proper job I'll repay the loan and get the house back.

JASMINDER'S MOTHER: Who knows when you'll find a job, *putr*? The agent had said you'll start earning within a month. Forget about the fees, you can't even afford your expenses.

JASMINDER: That's because these Australians don't like turbaned Sikhs doing front-end jobs. But once I get my degree in software engineering I'll get a *proper* job in a big company.

JASMINDER'S MOTHER: We are trying, *putr*, you focus on your studies. *Wahe guru sab theek karange.*

CUT TO THE PRESENT

JASMINDER: *Biji*, my grandmother, imagines my grandfather's spirit lives in our Gurdaspur house. Grandfather had built the house with his own hands. His ancestral house in Pakistan had been burnt down during India's partition. He lost everything—his parents and little brother were burnt alive with the house—but grandfather did not break down. He was a true Sikh, a fearless lion like we Sikhs are. He crossed the Pakistan border, lived in refugee camps and finally settled down in Gurdaspur. Our family has a strange destiny—we've been migrating for three generations, making new homes in new lands. This is my home now—this corner in a rented flat. Ranbeer found this flat for us. It was my second day at uni—I was looking for the library when Ranbeer walked up to me and solved all my problems.

ACT ONE 15

FLASHBACK

La Trobe University, eighteen months ago.

JASMINDER *looks lost as he talks to* RANBEER SINGH *(26).*

RANBEER: Have you found a place to stay?
JASMINDER: I saw some ads on the noticeboard, I am ...
RANBEER: *Phikr na kar yaar*, move in with us—we are looking for a flatmate.

CUT TO THE PRESENT

JASMINDER: Ranbeer became a housemate and an elder brother to me. We are all hard-up here—we go through hardships in the hope that we'll come out of it like Sarabjit uncle and grandfather. Whenever I feel bogged down I remind myself we are Sikhs—the warriors who fight to the end.

SCENE FIVE

Poorna's kitchen, Sunday morning.

POORNA *is chopping vegetables. He is holding the knife at the end. His hand moves in an awkward slow motion.*

POORNA: [*singing*] *Manasa Sancharare Brahmani*
　　　　Maanasa Sancharare ...
How do the chefs on TV shows chop vegetables in thirty seconds? I've been at it for one hour. Ah ... maybe singing is slowing down my speed.
　　He yawns.
It's because of the cricket match—otherwise I would have got up on time and finished the chopping by now. But how could I miss the Indo-Pak match, that too when India was winning—*dho daalaa sancharare.*
　　POORNA'S *phone rings.*
SHASHI: Hi, Poorna mate.
POORNA: Shashi?
SHASHI: Do you want me to pick up Coke on the way?
POORNA: Aren't you early for lunch? It's only eleven.
SHASHI: I have to reach the office by one o'clock.

POORNA: What's wrong with you—you can't work on a Sunday?
SHASHI: Don't tell me you haven't started cooking yet? I knew you wouldn't wake up on time.
POORNA: You should have told me you are coming early—*biryani* takes time.
SHASHI: Use a shortcut, Poorna mate. See ya.

SHASHI *disconnects.* POORNA *chops vegetables.*

POORNA: Shashi is crazy—he wants a shortcut for everything. How am I supposed to cook *biryani* in half an hour? What do I do—what do I do? Let me check with *amma* … she hates shortcuts but she knows everything about Indian cooking.

POORNA *calls up his* MOTHER *(47) in Hyderabad.*

POORNA'S MOTHER: Poorna!
POORNA: *Ella unaru, amma?*
POORNA'S MOTHER: Thank God you called.
POORNA: *Amma*, do you know how to make instant *biryani*?
POORNA'S MOTHER: Chinna and *nana* had a big fight last night. Your father's so anxious—can you call Chinna, he's not taking our call.
POORNA: What did they fight over this time?
POORNA'S MOTHER: Chinna's so adamant to do that ladies' course but your father said he's not paying the fees.
POORNA: *Arrey, amma*, talk to *nana*. He can't force Chinna to study engineering. Isn't he happy at least one of his sons is an engineer?
POORNA'S MOTHER: But for Chinna to do ladies' jobs!
POORNA: Everyone does everything these days, *amma*.
POORNA'S MOTHER: In our circle even girls work for banks and IT companies. They are not plucking women's eyebrows.
POORNA: What course are we talking about?
POORNA'S MOTHER: Beautician! A Telugu Brahmin boy waxing women's legs *chi chi*—how shameful.
POORNA: Beautician!
POORNA'S MOTHER: Only you can help your brother—call him to Australia and influence him to do something worthwhile.
POORNA: *Amma* please, it's not so easy. Shashi and Shiva are also working hard to get the job. It's tough competition.
POORNA'S MOTHER: I'll pray for you at Balaji temple, God has full power.

POORNA: It's *nana*'s idea, isn't it?
POORNA'S MOTHER: Not just your father, I want it too. You should try, for Chinna's sake.
POORNA: Don't worry, *amma*, Chinna is a smart boy, he'll do something big. Okay 'bye, I've to cook now, *selavu*.

He disconnects the phone.

Chinna, you can't do this to me. *Uuf*, Shashi and Shiva will be here any minute—I'll have to do a takeaway now. I've been eating pizza for one whole month.

SCENE SIX

Sonali's living room, night.
SONALI *is applying nail varnish. A red dress is spread on the couch.*

SONALI: [*singing*] *Meri desi look*
Meri desi look
meri desi look pe mar gaye, gore gore chokre
meri desi look pe mar gaye, gore gore chokre
Aussie guys are crazy about my *desi* looks la la la la la la la la la la ...

She admires her hands.

Red is my colour, it brings out the fire in me. Wait till he sees me in red lipstick. He's *tou* gonna faint. If only I could afford a salon—I need a sexy hairstyle tonight. You don't date guys like Andrew every day. Andrew's really really nice. He has deep blue eyes, just like Ricky—and he grins just like Ricky, he must have had wavy hair just like Ricky—it's receding now. I reckon he's forty/forty-two, but he's a good catch. He's educated, classy and he even reads books—a guy straight out of a Hollywood film—tall, white and handsome. It's 'luck by chance'—he had come to our store to buy a gift for his daughter. I helped him select a nice dress, but it turned out one size small. So he had to come back the next day to exchange it and that's when we got talking ...

FLASHBACK

The women's dress section in a large store.

ANDREW *(43) is making up his mind about a dress.*

ANDREW: I reckon it's the right size.

SONALI: Just give me a buzz if you want to change it or maybe I can call you up tomorrow! What's your number?

ANDREW: Thanks, but I'll come down—I live close by.

SONALI: Wow, which street?

ANDREW *steps back, surprised at her blatant advances.*

CUT TO THE PRESENT

SONALI: I could tell he was interested—the way he was checking me out and all that. He didn't give his phone number and walked out of the store as if I hadn't happened. But he couldn't resist the 'Sonali magic'. He called up the shop today and we're going out tonight. All my aunties used to say, 'Sonali knows how to *fasao* guys'. *Fasao* means trap. *Dilliwalli* aunties think any Delhi girl can *fasao* any Australian boy, but it's not so easy. All my cousins will die of an inferiority complex when they find out I have a new *Australian* boyfriend.

She pours a small drink in a glass, drinks.

I need a drink to boost my confidence. It's six months since I dated a guy. Will he like me? Will he like me enough to become serious? Will he be serious enough to commit? Will the commitment be good enough to last? There are so many ifs and buts. His case is a bit complicated—two kids from the first marriage. But never mind, it's too early to worry about these complications, it's only our first date.

A phone beep.

It's him. 'Be there in five minutes.' Five minutes! I'm not even dressed.

She tries to slip the dress over her head.

Down-down-down—hold my breath—another push—down-down—oh—

The dress rips.

Nooo—my red dress! What am I going to wear now? I should have suspected I had gained five kilos. Oh, *ma*, how will I *fasao* him without my red dress!

SCENE SEVEN

Jasminder's flat, day.

FLASHBACK

JASMINDER: I really wanted to go, Ranbeer *paaji*, but I had a terrible headache and no-one even bothered to give me a cup of tea. Everyone is in such a rush in this city, nobody would notice if you died in your sleep.

RANBEER: But, Jassi, why didn't you call up your boss and explain that you had to take a day off because you were sick? At least he wouldn't have fired you!

JASMINDER: Ranbeer *paaji*, I told him yesterday I was running high fever, but he doesn't care. He would have thrown me out even if I had called up. Your boss is an Indian—it's easy for you to take a day off.

RANBEER: So you think driving a taxi is fun? Do you think it's fun to do night shifts with drunk passengers abusing you at the back? And what happens when you ask them to pay up ...

He punches JASMINDER *without hurting him.*

If a *gora* says, 'Don't you get split ends and lice, mate? What's it like wearing the same turban again and again?' You *laugh*. You don't tell them, 'Shut up! It's a fucking stupid joke.'

CUT TO THE PRESENT

JASMINDER *ties a turban around his forehead.*

JASMINDER: My headache has got worse since Ranbeer scolded me this morning. On a rough day like this I need my mother's *masala* tea—a sure-shot remedy for headache.

He fills a pan with water to make masala *tea.*

I am not tough like Ranbeer. He can handle bad weather and rough situations. I can't do rough jobs. I had applied for a job at a store but they said my English is not up to the mark. It's not as if I can't speak English—I have taken coaching from 'British Speaking Centre', the best English school in Gurdaspur.

FLASHBACK

Gurdaspur, the British Speaking Centre, back in the day.

A TEACHER *(22) is teaching English to Punjabi country boys.*

TEACHER: *Pehle te zuban nou lacheela bunaao, hun Punjabi English eich bolange—oouu—eeee-aaae-saaa-haaa.*

JASMINDER *repeats after the* TEACHER.

JASMINDER: *Oouu—eeee-aaee-saaa-haaa. Pur* madam *ji, w*hy are we learning English language in Punjabi?

TEACHER: If you ask so many questions, Jassi, you'll never learn English—now pay attention and follow the instructions.

CUT TO THE PRESENT

JASMINDER *pours tea into a glass. Drinks.*

JASMINDER: Back in Gurdaspur people think once you enter a foreign country you can do some *jugaad* and settle down there. All they want to do is to settle down—not study, not have a career path—just settle down. *Jugaad* is being street smart the Indian way. Fools! *Jugaads* work only in Punjab, here you need money. They have no idea how expensive it is to live here—not even those immigration agents. Agents show you the websites of colleges where you see a huge campus, modern labs and the promise of a good life.

FLASHABCK

Gurdaspur, an office, back in the day.

An eager Punjabi IMMIGRATION AGENT *(42) is convincing* JASMINDER'S FATHER *(60).*

AGENT: Don't worry, Bauji, the boys I sent abroad are happily settled. Cunadaa, Englaand, Umerica *te* Australia. *Te* Jassi is a gem of a boy. No smoking, no drinking, no girls—expenses only three hundred dollars a month.

CUT TO THE PRESENT

JASMINDER: Three hundred dollars, my foot! First week was the toughest—I was multiplying every dollar with fifty-five rupees. When the dollar goes up, my food rations go down. I can live on rice and potatoes—that's not a problem. Besides, I get to eat butter chicken when Mohit brings leftovers from the Indian restaurant he works in. The biggest problem is rent.

FLASHBACK

Jasminder's flat, two days ago.

RANBEER: Hey, Jassi, Mohit is moving out next week—we'll have to pay a hundred dollars each till we find a new flatmate.

JASMINDER: But, Ranbeer *paaji*, I can't even afford eighty dollars a week.

RANBEER: *O yaar,* your money crisis never ends—*chal koi nahin.* Let's squeeze in more boys.

JASMINDER: Can we fit six mattresses in this room?

RANBEER: It's not a room, it's a bloody hall! Fifteen square metres! We can fit in as many mattresses as we want to.

JASMINDER: *Tusi great ho, paaji,* you always find solutions to my problems.

RANBEER: We can make it even better. Let's sleep in shifts—one mattress, two men.

CUT TO THE PRESENT

JASMINDER: If we sleep in shifts the rent can come down to thirty dollars. I can find a job or do some *jugaad* to pay the bills, but I still don't have the money to pay the fees. If only *biji* agrees to mortgage our Gurdaspur house … *Wahe guru,* please work out a solution for me.

SCENE EIGHT

Melbourne CBD, a tram stop.

POORNA *is waiting for his tram. He paces up and down, occasionally checking the display monitor.*

POORNA: Shashi and Shiva refused to come out for lunch. They have been working twelve hours nonstop. I can't work like that—I need a break. Shashi has changed—it's not just a change of *talam*, it's his soul.

FLASHBACK

Melbourne CBD, Poorna's office, morning, the same day.

POORNA: Hey, Shashi, let's go out for lunch.

SHASHI: I am not hungry—you guys carry on.

POORNA: Shiva's not hungry either. He feels like eating chips today.
SHASHI: Chips, my ass! I won't let him snatch my job—it's getting dirtier by the day.
POORNA: What's wrong with you two—we were friends, remember—*mates*!
SHASHI: I deserve this job—I've worked my ass off.
POORNA: We've all worked our asses off.
SHASHI: Yeah, yeah, yeah, I know but—you don't want this job, do you?
POORNA: I don't know ... my parents—
SHASHI: Good—that's one less.
POORNA: But are you sure you want to live here? Has anyone ever talked to you in this office—as in *talked*? Not 'Hi, beautiful day' kind of talk.
SHASHI: Why will they talk to us, they don't even talk to their parents.
POORNA: Don't you want to chat to friends?
SHASHI: I am not here to make friends. I am here to make big money and for that I need to move up fast, really fast.
POORNA: Don't you miss home? Don't you long for the sounds of Hyderabad—the call of the *koyal*, the ring of the temple bells, the *azaan*, the song of the hawkers, horns and hooters—oh, Hyderabad is so musical.

CUT TO THE PRESENT

POORNA *moves from the flashback to the tram stop in a seamless transition.*

POORNA: I need the noise, the madness of Hyderabad. I need my kind of people around—the people who believe in Rahu *kalam*, who match horoscopes before marrying, who go to a special Balaji temple before their visa interview at the American Embassy, who pray to a different god on different days of the week, who are excitable, loud, superstitious and crazy like me ... even at the tram stop I can't stop thinking of Hyderabad. Who's that—?

    POORNA *has been talking to himself. A tall* AUSTRALIAN MAN *(33) at the tram stop charges at him.*

AUSTRALIAN MAN: You were looking at me!
POORNA: Yes? No no no no, I was looking at the ...

AUSTRALIAN MAN: Don't you stare at me!

POORNA: There's been some kind of a misunderstanding, mate.

AUSTRALIAN MAN: I am not your mate, you shit-for-brains wanker.

The MAN *comes close, towering over and intimidating* POORNA. POORNA *moves back a few steps.*

POORNA: I didn't look at you, sir—I was looking for my tram and maybe for ten seconds I turned … *arere*, my *talam* …

The MAN *blocks* POORNA*'s way.* POORNA *realises his tram has arrived, passengers are boarding.* POORNA *waves at the tram to stop.*

AUSTRALIAN MAN: Talk to me in English—you freaky *talam*.

POORNA *skirts the* MAN, *chases the tram.*

POORNA: Side—get aside, I have to go … my traaam—hey stop—stoop the tram! Stop!

He stops running. He looks at the MAN *who is glowering at him and then at the road ahead—no sign of his tram.*

I better run away before this man kills me. *O Bhagwan*, protect me from the evil forces of this city.

POORNA *runs for his life.*

SCENE NINE

Sonali's living room, night.

SONALI *stumbles into her living room—she's drunk. She's shivering in a short dress. She fumbles with switches to turn on the heating.*

SONALI: God, I hate Melbourne winter—the house is freezing. My landlady's such a bitch, she refused to install a new heating unit. Whenever I demand something she threatens to increase the rent.

FLASHBACK

LANDLADY: Of course, dear, we can fix the heating. I am sure you can afford to pay a little extra money for comfort. And really, Indians have the best jobs these days.

SONALI *wraps herself in the blanket/shawl lying on the sofa.*

CUT TO THE PRESENT

SONALI: [*shivering*] Sure, I have the best job in the city—God knows, I have no money to blow up in pubs—but this house is so cold and the pub was so much warmer. If Andrew was in town I could have gone out with him, but he's such a slippery eel. Last weekend he was with his kids, this weekend he's skiing with his friends. He's been playing hot and cold after our first date—though it was a perfect date. He paid me compliments and he even picked up the bill—that's one thing Australian men don't do easily. And then he dropped me home ...

FLASHBACK

A street, night.

In mellow light, SONALI *talks in a seductive tone.* ANDREW *has his hands in his pockets, but he is enjoying the flirtation.*

SONALI: Why don't you come up for drinks, Andrew?
ANDREW: No, babe ... I got to drive back.
SONALI: Coffee is safe.
ANDREW: Not quite ...

> SONALI *grabs* ANDREW *by the waist. His hands are still in his pockets.*

CUT TO THE PRESENT

SONALI: He started with a reluctant kiss, but that was only at the start. He was quick and efficient with the rest of the business. He hasn't asked me out again and I don't want to chase him. If you call up an Australian guy more than once he thinks you are hitting on him. I am not mad about Andrew but everyone needs someone. No-one is interested in me except my mother. She's the only one who calls me. She keeps going on and on ...
SONALI'S MOTHER: Don't waste your life in Melbourne, *beta*, you can't work in a shop all your life. Look at your sister, she's a university topper. Even your *brother* is a graduate. I can't keep sending you money for the rest of your life. Why don't you finish your graduation, or do a course in fashion designing or jewellery making? You have such a good taste in clothes and jewellery. We can pay your college fees, but you have to come back to Delhi and convince your father that you are serious about your education and career.

ACT ONE

SONALI: Hunh—my mother thinks I can rewind my life. She's so naive—all my aunts and cousins are laughing at me. The whole world knows Ricky walked out on me—his profile picture is with his fat, ugly girlfriend. I can't believe he left me for that cheap bitch. Ricky and I had moved into this house together—everything was perfect for six months.

FLASHBACK

Sonali's living room, six months earlier.

RICKY *(28) is packing his bag.* SONALI *is sitting on the floor. She looks devastated.*

RICKY: I need a little space, babe, I want to hang out with my old mates.
SONALI: But we drink beer, we watch footy. We can do all the things you used to do with your flatmates.
RICKY: I hate watching footy with people who don't understand the game.
SONALI: I can sign up for footy classes if you like.

CUT TO THE PRESENT

SONALI: Ricky moved in with a high school girl—there's always a younger girl out there. Martha, the lonely Italian woman next door, had warned me about Australian men.
MARTHA: [66] Australian men want their women to get drunk and flooze around. If you are a woman of dignity like you and me, you stay within your four walls and work. Live alone and work.
SONALI: The day I left home I thought I was flying out of a cage. When I saw pigeons flying over our heads at Delhi airport I thought how far would these birds go if they decided to fly out? But you get tired of flying ...

She looks for wine.

Where's the bottle from last night—I couldn't have finished it? I can't even buy more wine—I reached the limit on my card today. *Ma* promised to send me money this week—why's she taking so long? She has no idea how I struggle for every cent.

She is anxious, calls India. SONALI'S BROTHER *takes the call.*

Ma?

BROTHER: *Haan, Sonali beta*, we don't love you anymore.
SONALI: Shut up and give the phone to *Ma*!
BROTHER: She goes to bed by eight.
SONALI: Wake her up—this is urgent.
BROTHER: Are you drunk?
SONALI: Are you crazy?
BROTHER: Keep it up, sister—you are on your way to becoming an Aussie.
SONALI: Do you ever talk sense?
BROTHER: Sure—Monali is going to London School of Economics. Dad has paid her fees cash down. He doesn't want Monali to work as a salesgirl in a shop.

He giggles.

SONALI *disconnects the phone.*

SONALI: Why do I have to try so hard—do I want the wrong things? I didn't come to Melbourne to become a drunkard and flooze around. I'll die of a heartache here—you have to be like Martha to survive in Melbourne—*fierce* and *strong*.

SCENE TEN

Jasminder's flat.

JASMINDER *is throwing his clothes into a suitcase. There's a heap of clothes on his mattress.*

JASMINDER: Squeeze, Jassi, squeeze. Come what may, you have to squeeze all the clothes into this suitcase. This is the third shelf I am clearing this week—isn't it amazing how much we can contract? This place seems crowded, but it's quite lonely. You are always alone here whereas in Gurdaspur people don't leave you alone.

He realises the heap won't fit into the suitcase. He takes them out, folds the clothes and puts them back.

O yaar ... I should have folded these clothes before putting them in. I have to make space for the new guys. We've found new flatmates and a man to share my bed. I haven't seen him though. Ranbeer has worked out a smart arrangement—the man pays me twenty dollars a week and I keep out of his way.

ACT ONE

FLASHBACK

Jasminder's flat, two days earlier.

RANBEER: Hey, Jassi, you better be out by ten. The guy wants to sleep as soon as he comes in.

JASMINDER: But, Ranbeer, my classes start at two o'clock.

RANBEER: *O Jassi yaar*, spend some time in the library. You better work hard, *teri* percentage *vi* down *chal rahi hai*.

CUT TO THE PRESENT

JASMINDER *sits on the overstuffed suitcase to shut it. He locks it while sitting on it.*

JASMINDER: *Oye bund ho ja khotya*, shut it, shut it, done. This is 'Made in Punjab' suitcase—solid stuff, not like those delicate Chinese bags which break at the airport. My father bought this suitcase when I was coming to Melbourne. *Bebe* packed the whole kitchen in this—utensils, pickles, biscuits, rusks, *mathis*, *laddoos*, medicines, hair oil, towels, clothes, turbans, shoes and … everything fitted in so well. I was nervous the day I left home. I was flying for the first time and that too out of the country. I had never been to a foreign country. *Bebe* was more nervous than me—her only child was leaving her nest. She kissed me on the forehead—they say mothers kiss you on the forehead to awaken your third eye. She must have known you need more than two eyes to survive in Melbourne. She worries so much. I think of her and she calls me—

JASMINDER*'s phone rings. His* MOTHER *is on the line.*

Hello, *bebe*, did you talk to *grandmother*?

JASMINDER'S MOTHER: *Aaho putr*, everything is sorted—*biji* has agreed to mortgage the house.

JASMINDER: When will you send the money?

JASMINDER'S MOTHER: Speed Post takes time, *putr*—we have sent the papers to England.

JASMINDER: What has Sarabjit uncle got to do with this?

JASMINDER'S MOTHER: It's a small formality—we only need a no-objection certificate from him. Don't worry, you'll get the money. Just focus on your studies. This call is getting expensive. *Changa phir, dhyan karin.*

JASMINDER'S MOTHER *disconnects the line.*

JASMINDER: I knew *biji* would say yes—I am her favourite grandchild. When I was a child she used to tell me the stories of our gurus. She would say, 'Never lose faith, Jassi. God wants us to be brave and fearless, just like your grandfather. A true Sikh.'
Naik na ran te muri chale nidar havey ghai
Gir gir parei patang te bare barangan jai.

SCENE ELEVEN

Melbourne CBD, Poorna's office.

POORNA: Good morning, boss.
BOSS: Hi, Poorna. I wanted to chat to you about your friends. They cc me in on every email—I don't have time for their finger pointing.
POORNA: Yeah ...
BOSS: You are a nice bloke, Poorna. But your friends ... I need people who can work in a team. Who's fault is it—who's not doing their job, Shashi or Shiva?
POORNA: You.
BOSS: Easy, mate.
POORNA: Who started this competition—the best guy stays?
BOSS: That's how things work here. You are not being fired, we are only sending you back to our office in your country.
POORNA: It's not about going back, it's about losing a race.
BOSS: This could go against all of you, Poorna.
POORNA: Well, I don't care.

POORNA leaves in a huff. Picks up his laptop bag and umbrella and walks to the station. He is restless and agitated.

SCENE TWELVE

Melbourne, Flagstaff Station, evening, the same day.

POORNA *is outside the station. He checks his platform on the display monitor, finds his ticket, swipes it, goes past the boom gate, runs down the escalator to the platform.*

POORNA: Where's my— platform three—four minutes—just in time! *Myki myki myki*—quick quick-quick ... This umbrella slows me down, bloody Melbourne weather! Excuse me—sorry sorry—thank you. [*Out of breath*] Just on time—just on time. *Uuf*, this is crazy. I am forever chasing trains and trams. Shashi starts calling me within ten minutes of my leaving the office. He wants me to start working on the train. Everyone keeps pushing me. I have been working nonstop. There are no pauses, no breaks. I have completely lost my *talam*. All I hear is the ring of mobile phones, the noise of escalators, platform announcements and the trains squealing on the tracks. Where's the *koyal*, where's the ring of temple bells, where's Carnatic music, where's my mother's voice? I feel spaced out. I haven't slept for a week. Not tonight. I am going to shut down the laptop, switch off the phone and *sleep*.

He is pacing up and down on a nearly empty platform. JASMINDER *is waiting for his train.* POORNA*'s phone rings.*

Shashi? [*Taking the call*] Chapundi— No, I am not discussing this again— Oh really, I screwed up your career? And what were you trying to do when you were writing those emails?— You think I can't read between lines. 'That's a smug report, Shiva.' 'Poorna, please back up your analysis with data.' Do I look like a dumb Jimmy?

JASMINDER *notices* POORNA. *He also sees* SONALI *walking onto the platform with a coffee.* POORNA *does not pay attention to the others.*

If you had your way you would have put me and Shiva on the first flight to India— Don't worry, we are all going back together on the same flight— Thanks to you, yes, thanks to you— No, I didn't mess anything, you did— Cut it, cut it, I have to go— No, I am not coming back to the office, I am going home—

The sound of an approaching train. JASMINDER *has been watching* POORNA. SONALI *is waiting on the other end, drinking coffee, surfing the internet on her phone.*

What?! How dare you! How dare you say that, you son-of-a—shiiit!

POORNA *loses his balance, his phone slips. He trips over his umbrella and falls down with his heavy laptop bag.* JASMINDER *leaps towards him.*

JASMINDER: *O Vekha ke ...*

JASMINDER *tries to catch* POORNA *in vain. The train is speeding in.* JASMINDER *waves at the train to stop.* POORNA *tries to get up but his foot is stuck. The laptop bag is still on his back.* SONALI *has realised something is amiss. She throws her cup, rushes towards* JASMINDER.

JASMINDER: Stop the train— Stooooop ...!

SONALI: Hey you, step back!

JASMINDER *runs towards the train, waving his arms, signalling it to stop.* SONALI *sees* POORNA *on the tracks.* SONALI *is horrified.* SONALI *runs to the other end looking for help.*

JASMINDER: Stop—there's a man on the tracks! Stop!

SONALI: Help help! Is somebody there—help us please!

The train wheels screech—the train halts. JASMINDER *freezes in shock,* SONALI *stops.*

Blackout.

END OF ACT ONE

ACT TWO

SCENE ONE

Sonali's living room, night, the same day.
SONALI is wrapped in a blanket. She is sitting on the sofa with a book. But she is too distracted to read. Sighs, tries to read again. Gives up.

SONALI: I don't want to be alone tonight. There are days you need people—even if it's a presence.
  Her phone rings. She answers.
  [*On the phone*] I have been calling you all evening, Andrew.
ANDREW: Hi, babe, I was in meetings—anything urgent?
SONALI: I need to talk to you.
ANDREW: Ooh ...
SONALI: Can you come over tonight?
ANDREW: Ummn ... my dog ... he has an ear infection, but we can talk on the phone.
SONALI: I am feeling low—my heart is sinking ...
ANDREW: Just take a tranquiliser.
SONALI: There was an accident   ANDREW: Where?
  at the station—I was right
  there ...
  ANDREW surfs the internet on his laptop.
SONALI: I threw up—I couldn't   ANDREW: Is it on the net ...?
  stand the sight ...
SONALI: The train came straight   ANDREW: Flagstaff?
  into him—his legs were ripped
  from his body onto the tracks.
  I puked on the platform ...
SONALI: I don't want to go to that   ANDREW: Why isn't the video
  station ever.   on YouTube ...?
SONALI: I can't get over the sight—there was blood everywhere, on the man, on the tracks and his legs ...

ANDREW: Sleep it off, honey.
SONALI: Wait, wait, wait a second—!

ANDREW *has disconnected.*

Bloody YouTube maniac. I should have called up my mother—she's the only one who cares.

SONALI *calls India.*

SONALI'S FATHER: *Kaun hai*? Hello ... who's on the line? Speak up.

SONALI *cannot find her voice. A muffled squeak:*

SONALI: Dad ...
SONALI'S FATHER: Sonali? *Haraamzadi!*
SONALI'S FATHER: You're always after our money.
SONALI'S FATHER: Stop calling your mother, I don't want to hear your voice in my house ...

SONALI: Papa—
SONALI: No, Papa ... no—
SONALI: Dad—listen—please ...

SONALI'S FATHER *disconnects the phone.*

SONALI: Dad, please! I have no-one. No-one to even talk to. Nothing is working for me in this city—I don't know what I'm doing here? What am I doing with my life?

SCENE TWO

Jasminder's flat, the same night.

RANBEER *turns on the light.* JASMINDER *is sitting on his mattress, sobbing.*

JASMINDER: Ranbeer *paaji*?
RANBEER: *Light te on kar lya kar yaar* ... What happened?
JASMINDER: *Bada ganda accident vekhya aj*—Indian *munda si*. He fell on the tracks and his legs were completely ...

JASMINDER *sobs.*

RANBEER: *Zyadah tension na kar*—you'll fall sick if you stress too much.
JASMINDER: I was behind him—he was talking on the phone. I heard the train and he saw it too. And then suddenly he lost his balance. He stretched his hand—I tried to reach him but he went down so fast.

I should have moved faster. It's my fault. A true Sikh would have saved him.

RANBEER: Good, you didn't get too close to him—he could have taken you down. It's physics—the low static pressure created by the train pulls you in. You couldn't have saved him, thank God you saved yourself—you are the only child of your parents. *Koi nahin*—we'll go to the Gurudwara on Sunday.

> JASMINDER *does not respond—his mind is elsewhere.* RANBEER *notices/smells the pile in the kitchen sink.*
>
> *Beat.*

Jassi *yaar*, the sink is full and the whole place is stinking. Can you do the dishes please? I am going to pull up these new guys—they keep the house so badly.

> RANBEER *exits to the toilet.*

JASMINDER: Did I escape death? Was it my turn to die?

SCENE THREE

Melbourne, a hospital ICU ward, seven days later.

POORNA *is restless. A* NURSE *(27) comes in. She switches off the 'nurse call button' that has been ringing. She is holding a card.*

NURSE: Hello, Mr Poornachandra. It's day seven, you're looking great.
POORNA: I want to speak with my friends.
NURSE: They'll see you during the hospital visiting hours—do you need something?
POORNA: Phone—I need a phone.
NURSE: We are not allowed phones in the ICU.
POORNA: I want to talk to my parents …

> *The* NURSE *hangs the card by the bedside. The card says 'NIL BY MOUTH'.*

What's on that card?

NURSE: 'Nil by mouth'—you are fasting after a light lunch.
POORNA: Are they taking me to the operation theatre?
NURSE: Your surgeon will explain on his rounds.
POORNA: They can't stitch my legs back, can they?

The NURSE *draws the curtain so that* POORNA *doesn't disturb other patients. She speaks in a hush.*

NURSE: You'll feel better when you move out of the ICU—gets a bit oppressive here.

POORNA: It's not the ICU, it's my life that is oppressive.

The NURSE *glances over the medicine chart.*

NURSE: No antideps? I'll send a referral to the psychiatrist, okay?

The NURSE *notes it in the file. Leaves.* POORNA *is getting more restless.*

POORNA: I don't need a psychiatrist—I want my legs back! Where are my legs—did they bring them to the hospital—I have to go to the station ...

SCENE FOUR

Sonali's living room, day.

A yoga mat is in the centre of the room. The couch has been moved to the side. SONALI *is doing Surya Namaskar (yoga).*

SONALI: One-two-three-four-five-return-four-three-two-one-stop. Oh! Surya Namaskar is so invigorating, it's helping me get on with my life. I was slipping into the blues after I saw the accident. Andrew's coldness, money crunch, weight gain, hair loss—everything was weighing me down. I couldn't sleep—every night I had scary dreams. My GP gave me pills that make you feel good about your life, but pills can't replace people. In India everyone helps you tide over bad experiences. Even your servants cheer you up. And then one morning I saw bags under my eyes—*ugly* red bags. That was my wake-up call. No pills, no junk food, no alcohol and no *men*. I am on a complete makeover program for my heart, body and soul. The detoxification diet I follow is supposed to throw out all the shit in your system. The diet is already working—I've not had a better bowel movement since I came here. I have also signed up for 'How to heal your heart *chakra*' program, [*sighing*] a free online treatment for *heartbreaks*. The lady who runs the program is so motivating— [*sighing*] she has suffered more heartbreaks than me. I start my day with *pranayam*.

ACT TWO

Baba, the yoga guru, says throw the negativity out with every breath. *She starts with gentle breathing and then her breathing picks up pace.*

Ooom … Goodness in, shit out—goodness in, shit out … Goodness in—*saale, kuttey, kamine, haramzade,* bastards—get out, get the fuck out … *Ooooooom* … I am beginning to feel more positive because of yoga … I am learning to face my past and plan my future. *Oom* … I will finish my graduation and focus on my career *Ooom* … I have the courage to face the world. I don't give a shit about what my cousins think. *Oom* … They can laugh at me for all I care, Bitches! *Ooooom* … [*Sighing*] Had it not been for so much meditation and yoga I would have freaked out last week. I had gone to the temple because I was feeling low that day, and what did I see there, my ex-husband with his newlywed wife. They looked happy together. Their happiness made me more miserable. I could have lived happily with Vivek if I had tried, but how could have I known that Ricky was such a mean bastard? I am done chasing men. I am going to going to live my life on my own—

ANDREW *calls.*

Andrew's call! [*On the phone*] Hiii! Long time.
ANDREW: Hey, babe, are you at the shop?
SONALI: It's my day off, I am doing yoga—
ANDREW: Great. I am on my way to your shop—
SONALI: Are you at the store!
ANDREW: I'll be there in half an hour, but don't worry I'll ask someone to help me—
SONALI: No no no no. All the girls are useless and they don't know your taste. I am coming—
ANDREW: No no no—please don't …

SONALI *puts on a jacket as she talks.*

SONALI: It's alright, I am on my way—two minutes.

She disconnects the phone.

A message from the universe! Just when I was thinking of becoming a nun Andrew called. It's not a coincidence, God has a plan for me. A beautiful, romantic plan.

SCENE FIVE

Jasminder's flat.

JASMINDER *is reading a text book. He is distracted and anxious. His long hair is tangled. He throws the book on the floor.*

JASMINDER: I don't know what's wrong with me, I have forgotten everything I had learnt. I have an exam tomorrow but everything is jumbled up in my mind.
    He drinks some water.
    Sarabjit uncle has refused to sign the papers. He told my grandmother, 'Jassi will never find a job in Melbourne, all the jobs have gone to India and China. Don't risk the house—it's our father's blessing.' Blessing, my foot! Uncle has done nothing for that goddamn house or for his father. I was hoping Ranbeer would help ...

FLASHBACK

Jasminder's flat, two days earlier.

RANBEER: How could you trust a man who used to gift you his family's castaways? Shows how much your uncle cares.
JASMINDER: We didn't think uncle would say no, my father has done so much for him. And uncle doesn't need our house—he has a big bungalow in England.
RANBEER: Now what?
JASMINDER: I don't know—maybe I'll take a year off from university, work somewhere and save money for the fees. I am halfway through graduation—I am sure I can manage the rest of the course. I talked to the admin staff ...
RANBEER: There's no way you can work here legally.
JASMINDER: Sarabjit uncle worked in England without a visa.
RANBEER: That's history—twenty years back people could disappear, not anymore. They'll hunt you down.
JASMINDER: I'll hide somewhere ...
RANBEER: Where will you hide—in the toilet? Do you have the balls to face an interrogation?
JASMINDER: I'll give them some excuse—anything is better than going back.

ACT TWO

RANBEER: Do you want to end in a detention centre? You think you can handle that shit?

JASMINDER: So many Indians manage to come out of detention, there has to be a—

RANBEER: [*becoming impatient*] Don't screw up your life, Jassi, detention is a nightmare. Just go back, you don't have a choice.

JASMINDER: What will I do in Punjab? All my friends in Gurdaspur will graduate next year, and what am I, a high school pass? I can't go back without a *degree, paaji*.

RANBEER *pushes* JASMINDER.

RANBEER: You can't stay here—this is not your grandmother's house. You need a visa to live in this country. I don't want police in this flat—my name's on the lease and I am not getting involved in your shit. Is that clear?

JASMINDER: I only want to finish my graduation—is that too much to ask? I have spent so much money, gone without food and medicines, lived on practically nothing—for what? Can I go back? No-one goes back, I go in circles and a circle is a zero. Bauji's money, my efforts, my mother's blessings, the time I spent here, the hardships I lived through, the nights of panic, the days of anxiety—everything becomes zero.

SCENE SIX

A room in the hospital.

POORNA *is in a wheelchair. The* NURSE *comes in.*

NURSE: Hello, Mr Poorna. Did you enjoy the walk?
POORNA: Walk—what a joke!
NURSE: Can I shift you back to your bed?
POORNA: I'm expecting a call—it's easier to reach the phone from the chair.
NURSE: No worries. Buzz me when you are done.

The NURSE *exits. The phone rings,* POORNA *reaches it with effort.*

POORNA: Hello.
POORNA'S MOTHER: How are you feeling, *babu*?

POORNA: What do you expect me to feel, *amma*? I am great.
POORNA'S MOTHER: Don't be disheartened, Poorna. Chinna is going to Sabrimala temple to pray for you—
POORNA: What's wrong with Chinna—he used to be a logical guy. You must have brainwashed him to do this crazy pilgrimage. You can't make him walk barefeet for forty days! It's atrocious.
POORNA'S MOTHER: Chinna has changed after this misfortune fell on us—he has been going to the temple every day. Once we bring you back he'll look after you. He will take you for physiotherapy, oil massage, and wherever you need to go. He has pledged to carry you to Sabrimala temple on his back—
POORNA: Stop! Please stop it, *amma*!

He breaks down, disconnects the phone.

If I go back to Hyderabad *amma* and *nana* will reduce me to an invalid and forsake Chinna to look after a disabled brother. I can't go back. God, why did I come here? The day I left home, *amma* had warned it was not a good time to travel. I mocked her, 'Offer a coconut at Balaji temple and things will be fine'. The planets are playing with my life. I have to take charge before they wreck Chinna's life.

A knock on the door. The BOSS *comes in.*

BOSS: Hi, Poorna, how are you today?
POORNA: Boss! I am—good. I went out for a … walk.
BOSS: Lovely … it's a beautiful day, isn't it?
POORNA: The doctor said I can start working—I need a new laptop.
BOSS: There's no rush—Shashi is managing everything. You should focus on your recovery.
POORNA: I need something to occupy myself with—I'm going crazy sitting alone.
BOSS: Watch TV—there are so many good shows on.
POORNA: Shiva was telling me about the new project. I have some ideas—
BOSS: Great, we'll discuss them after you are recovered.
POORNA: If you give me a laptop, I can mail them to you.
BOSS: Sure. You'll get a new laptop in Hyderabad. Mr Ganesha has created a new job for you in Hyderabad office—you can even work from home.
POORNA: But I haven't completed my work in Melbourne.

ACT TWO 39

BOSS: Shashi suggested, and I think he's right, that you join Hyderabad office straight away. Shashi will complete your work here.
POORNA: So I am not in the race for the Melbourne job?
BOSS: It's not official but ...
POORNA: You can't disqualify me because of my disability.
BOSS: Don't you think it'll be easier for you to live with your family in your own city?
POORNA: They are the reason I don't want to go back. I am sick of their sympathy. I want to work here—I can work twenty-four seven. India is a nightmare for disabled people. People like me have to live on others' mercy—we can't even use the public transport.
BOSS: Really—that's terrible. We'll discuss this later, Poorna ... I've to get back to office for a sales meeting. 'Bye—take care ...

The BOSS *pats* POORNA's *back. She starts to leave.*

POORNA: Just one more thing, boss ...
BOSS: Yes?
POORNA: You had asked, 'Who's at fault?' Do you still want to know?
BOSS: It's alright—you don't have to answer that now.
POORNA: Shashi's the one. He was lying about his work status. He was reporting more work than he had actually done and when the clients started complaining he blamed it on Shiva and me. Shashi is ambitious—he can pull down anyone to go up—even his boss.

The BOSS *does not react.*

Beat.

She exits.

SCENE SEVEN

Sonali's apartment, evening.
A chocolate cake is on the table. SONALI *blows out the candles.*

SONALI: [*singing*] Happy birthday to me
Happy birthday to me ...
Two candles for three decades! It's been a quiet day so far. Last birthday I was with Ricky—we had gone out for a candlelight dinner. But Ricky didn't even wish me this year. I called him up last night, hoping he'll want to meet me on my birthday—his girlfriend answered

the phone—'Get lost, bitch, don't call ma guy'. [*With a sigh*] I threw out all the negativity in the morning yoga session. *Ma* was the first one to wish me, my sister called me up, and the girls from work wished me. But no-one said, 'Let's go out, Sonali, you are alone'. In Delhi we used to celebrate our birthdays all day. My mother would cook my favourite dishes and my dad used to order a chocolate cake from the best shop in Delhi. I didn't want to break the ritual of eating a chocolate cake on my birthday, so ...

> *She cuts and eats the cake.*

Hmmn ... not bad. I'll have to finish it quickly—it's from the clearance stock. There's no-one to share the cake with—Andrew's gone—I *dumped* him. He said there had been a cultural misunderstanding. I had called him up last week ...

FLASHBACK

A few days ago.

SONALI: Why can't you meet me today, Andrew?
ANDREW: Sorry, babe, I am going out tonight.
SONALI: Who are you going out with?
ANDREW: Jeez.
SONALI: Are you seeing someone?
ANDREW: Hey, slow down ... I think there's been a cultural misunderstanding.

CUT TO THE PRESENT

SONALI: Fucking middle-aged user! He blocked my number. Bastard! How can there be a cultural misunderstanding? I am Australian—I know the place, I know its culture, I know its rhythm, this is the country of my soul, dammit. I am not a traditional Indian girl—I am an independent international woman. I live alone without a family or friends and it's freaking hard, I tell you. Being traditional was easy. Maybe I was wrong—maybe I shouldn't have flown out of the cage ... it was a safe sanctuary. Martha was right ...
MARTHA: Five weeks or five years, men always leave. Who needs love? Women like you and me don't need men.
SONALI: All I wanted was a beautiful life with a beautiful man, I followed my heart and this is where it has brought me. I was living in a delusion.

I don't need love, I don't need men, I just need a break ... from this vicious cycle of pain.

>SONALI *drinks.*

SCENE EIGHT

Jasminder's flat, evening.

>JASMINDER *is anxious.*

JASMINDER: Nothing is working out—Bauji tried talking to Sarabjit uncle but he is adamant. We can't mortgage the house without uncle's consent. Now even my grandmother believes I am a loser. What a drain I have been on my parents! Sarabjit uncle was right—I am a weak boy and there's no place for the weak in Melbourne. Why didn't I fall on the tracks that day—it would have solved everything. If I die, at least my parents will be free to live their life. Oh God! I am feeling cold again—every few days the fever comes back. Where did I keep the medicine?

>*He goes to the kitchen, opens a drawer, looks for the medicine.*

Who left the knife here? It almost cut my hand, such a sharp—

>*He takes out the knife, leaves it on the bench.*

What am I thinking? No no, I can't—

>*He considers picking up the knife. There's a moment of tension.*
>
>*Beat.*
>
>RANBEER *leaps at* JASMINDER *from behind.* RANBEER *takes* JASMINDER *by the arm, turning and twisting his arm behind his back.*

RANBEER: *Saale teri maa ki,* you didn't find a better place to kill yourself. I told you I don't want police in my house. Don't mess with me, Jassi—I won't take it. Get out of here and get lost.

>JASMINDER *runs out of the flat.* RANBEER *is overcome with guilt.*

O Jassi, *ruk,* wait!

>RANBEER *pulls out Jasminder's papers from his suitcase, makes a call.*

SCENE NINE

Melbourne, Flagstaff Station, Friday evening.

JASMINDER *stands on the edge of the platform. He's staring into the abyss. A train announcement is in progress.*

JASMINDER: Don't look at the train, don't look at the train, it's coming it's coming, look ahead, straight ahead—start counting—one two three four five …

He is sweating and of breath. The sound of an approaching train. His phone rings.

Beat.

Don't take the call, don't take the call—who's calling—don't listen to the phone, don't listen to the phone.

His phone stops ringing. The sound of the train is closing in.

Beat.

JASMINDER *resumes counting in a shaky voice, but the counting is quicker this time.*

Okay—good—one two three four—

The phone rings again.

—five six seven eight nine—who's calling me again and again?

He answers the phone.

[*On the phone*] Mother? Hello, *bebe*, why are you crying? I am fine—I said I am fine, yes I am safe. Ranbeer called you?

Beat.

I have to go, my train's here. 'Bye 'bye.

The train is already on the platform. JASMINDER *disconnects the phone. He knows his moment has passed. He avoids looking at people.*

SONALI *has got off the train. She drags two suitcases, has one backpack on her back and a purse on her arm. She struggles with her luggage. Wheel of one suitcase jams.* JASMINDER *sees her but* SONALI *looks away immediately. She tries to pull/fix the suitcase.*

ACT TWO 43

SONALI: Damn! Bloody Flagstaff Station. Everything goes wrong here. I have a flight in three hours and my suitcase is stuck—shit! [*To* JASMINDER] Hello, hello, can you give me a hand—he can't hear me or what—

She waves at JASMINDER. *He avoids her.*

[*Louder*] Help me please!

JASMINDER *turns when* SONALI *says 'please'.*

My suitcase is stuck.

JASMINDER *goes up to* SONALI *but avoids her eye.*

Can you fix it, please?

JASMINDER: I can try.

SONALI: I should have taken a taxi but I felt like taking the train from Flagstaff one last time. Call it nostalgia …

JASMINDER *examines the suitcase and the wheel. Tries to fix it.*

JASMINDER: It's the wheel.

SONALI: It just needs to hold till India.

JASMINDER: You are going to India! What about your job?

SONALI: Job—what job? Oh, jooob—I kicked the job.

JASMINDER: But you speak such good English, why did they kick you out?

SONALI: Excuse me! I didn't get kicked out, I chucked my job. I hated my boss. She was always bossing us, 'You can't drink on duty'. Balls! I threw the wine on her face and walked out.

JASMINDER: [*shocked*] You quit your job!

SONALI: I am not cut out for these no-brainer jobs. I was born to do big things.

JASMINDER: You quit your job!

SONALI: No more job shit for me! I am going to do a Bachelor's degree in Arts with a major in fashion design. For the next three years I am going to focus on my education and then I will work with a celebrity fashion designer and after I have gained some experience I will design wedding gowns with Indian embroidery and stonework. Mark my words—in less than ten years I will be rich and famous. [*With a sigh*] But it's not just for my career, I am going to India for my mother, she needs me. She's depressed because my sister moved to London and

typically, my father has no time for her. Besides, what's the big deal about Melbourne? Do you really think it's the most liveable—
JASMINDER: It's fixed.
SONALI: Wow, great! Thanks. Are you an engineer—hey, wait! Have I seen you somewhere? I could be wrong—these last few months have been so difficult—

JASMINDER *looks directly at* SONALI *for the first time and nods in acknowledgment.*

Beat.

JASMINDER: Platform three.
SONALI: O yes, the accident! You are the one who tried to save the Indian man! How did I miss it? You are so brave and fearless. A true *Sikh*. Thanks ... for the suitcase.
JASMINDER: 'Bye.

SONALI *and* JASMINDER *shake hands.* SONALI *pats his shoulder as she leaves. The words 'a true Sikh' have caught* JASMINDER. *He watches her go.*

SONALI *pauses to look at the platform one last time.*

Beat.

SONALI: Sometimes you need courage to just keep moving on.
JASMINDER: *'Naik na ran te muri chale nidar havey ghai,*
Gir gir parei patang te bare barangan jai.'
'They do not retract their steps from the battlefield and inflict wounds fearlessly,
Those who fall from their horses, the heavenly damsels go to wed them.'
A true *Sikh* I am.

SONALI *walks to the exit sign, crosses* POORNA.

POORNA *has come out of the lift. He's in a wheelchair.* SONALI *looks at him, shudders at the sight.* JASMINDER *leaves.*

POORNA *waits on the platform.*

He reads mail on his phone. There's no oil in his hair, no tika, not even earphones. He looks up to listen to the announcement.

POORNA: Fuck! They cancelled the train! I hate Flagstaff. Ttt. How will I mail the presentation in two hours? Let me ask Shiva to mail the data,

ACT TWO

then I can at least finish some work on the train. [*Typing*] That's one good habit I picked from Shashi—working on the train and writing mails on the platform. There's no time for cricket, not even music. I haven't spoken—

An incoming call.

Why's Shashi calling from Hyderabad?

He accepts the call.

[*On the phone*] Hey, Shashi. Can you mail the data in ten minutes?— You've slowed down, mate, I don't have thirty minutes— Not again— Come off it, Shashi, stop cursing the boss. She gave me the job because she wanted to help me— Yeah yeah yeah, I know she had promised you the job, but— What do you mean don't trust her, I don't trust anyone— Are you serious, I can't come back— Your voice is cracking— Hello, hello ...

The sound of a train.

Shit!

He looks around.

Beat.

Everyone says come back to Hyderabad. *Amma* pleads on the phone, *nana* writes sentimental mails, friends WhatsApp messages, but I am glad I didn't go back. Work keeps me going. Rageshwari got married last week, at least I didn't have to face her. I don't know if I belong in Melbourne, but I am getting used to it—all of it—the patter of rain, the rhythm of trains, fixed timetables, changing platforms, noisy trams, girls in bikinis, boys on skateboards, tall men, taller women, and someday I am sure I'll learn to sync with the Melbourne *talam*.

He looks around.

Beat.

He continues waiting on the platform.

Beat.

THE END

www.currency.com.au

Visit Currency Press' website now to:

- Buy your books online
- Browse through our full list of titles, from plays to screenplays, books on theatre, film and music, and more
- Choose a play for your school or amateur performance group by cast size and gender
- Obtain information about performance rights
- Find out about theatre productions and other performing arts news across Australia
- For students, read our study guides
- For teachers, access syllabus and other relevant information
- Sign up for our email newsletter

The performing arts publisher